Look Door, Get Key : A Guide to Writing Adventure Games

J. Hereford

For Tara.

iv

Contents

Introduction: Crossing the Threshold

Sometimes a door is just a door. Other times, it's a portal to a world of adventure. - Unknown

0.1 The Concept of Interactive Narratives

In the realm of storytelling, interactive narratives have emerged as a revolutionary force, challenging the traditional, linear approach to narrative construction. Rather than being passive recipients of a predetermined story, readers—or players, in the context of games—become active participants, shaping the narrative through their decisions and actions. This dynamic, participatory nature of interactive narratives endows them with an unparalleled power to engage, immerse, and resonate with audiences. As we embark on our exploration of this fascinating realm, let's begin by understanding what interactive narratives truly are and why they hold such significance in the world of storytelling.

Interactive narratives are a hybrid of traditional storytelling and gameplay, combining the narrative depth of literature with the interactive engagement of games. They offer a unique narrative experience, where the story unfolds differently based on the choices made by the player. Each decision opens up a new path, leading to a different outcome, making the narrative a dynamic, mutable entity. This fluidity of narrative structure is what sets interactive narratives apart from conventional, linear stories.

The power of interactive narratives lies not just in their novelty, but in their ability to reflect the complexity and unpredictability of real life. In life, as in interactive narratives, our choices shape our experiences and outcomes. They reflect our values, beliefs, and desires, making us active participants in our own life stories. This mirroring of life's complexity and dynamism is what makes interactive narratives a profoundly engaging and immersive storytelling medium.

0.2 Inspiration Behind the Book

The inspiration behind this book can be traced back to the acclaimed Netflix/Black Mirror series, Bandersnatch, particularly the symbolic prop book, 'Look Door, Get Key.' In the series, this book subtly guided the protagonist through a complex narrative maze, mirroring the intricate, choice-driven nature of interactive narratives. Like its fictional counterpart, this real-life 'Look Door, Get Key' aims to serve as a guide, not through a fictional narrative, but through the art and craft of creating interactive narratives. As we delve into the world of adventure games and interactive storytelling, we'll frequently draw parallels with elements from Bandersnatch, allowing us to explore these concepts in a familiar, relatable context.

In Bandersnatch, 'Look Door, Get Key' represented the protagonist's guide through the labyrinth of his own mind, a symbol of the many paths and choices that lay before him. It served as a metaphorical compass, pointing the way through a narrative landscape shaped by the protagonist's decisions. This book aims to play a similar role for its readers, illuminating the path to creating compelling, choice-driven narratives. By drawing upon elements from Bandersnatch, we can bring these abstract concepts to life, grounding them in a narrative that has captivated audiences worldwide.

However, this book is not merely a carbon copy of its fictional namesake. While the 'Look Door, Get Key' of Bandersnatch was a cryptic, metaphysical guide, this book aims to be a clear, practical, and comprehensive manual for creating interactive narratives. It's not just about drawing a map of the narrative landscape—it's about equipping readers with the tools they need to navigate that landscape, to craft their own unique, compelling interactive narratives. In this sense, while it draws inspiration from Bandersnatch, this 'Look Door, Get Key' is an entity unto itself, a guide for the real-world adventure of crafting interactive narratives.

0.3 The Role of Philosophy in Interactive Narratives

Interactive narratives are not just about the mechanics of choice and consequence; they're deeply intertwined with philosophical themes. The freedom to choose, the burden of consequences, the existential dilemmas—these are all fundamental aspects of our human experience, and interactive narratives bring them into sharp focus. Each choice a player makes, each path they tread, reflects not just a gaming strategy, but a philosophical stance. As we navigate the world of interactive narratives, we'll also delve into these underlying philosophical elements, uncovering the profound depths of this innovative storytelling medium.

The philosophical underpinnings of interactive narratives can be traced back to the age-old philosophical debates surrounding free will and determinism. In an interactive narrative, the player is seemingly granted the freedom to make choices, but these choices are, in fact, confined within the predetermined boundaries set by the game developers. This creates a unique interplay between freedom and constraint, mirroring the philosophical tension between free will and determinism. Exploring this tension offers a deeper understanding of the philosophical nuances inherent in interactive narratives.

Beyond the philosophical debate of free will and determinism, interactive narratives also engage with existential themes. Players are often confronted with existential dilemmas, forced to make choices that question their values, beliefs, and perceptions of reality. These existential elements are not mere embellishments; they are integral to the immersive, emotionally engaging experience that interactive narratives provide. As we delve deeper into the art of crafting interactive narratives, we'll explore how these philosophical and existential themes can be woven into the fabric of our stories, enhancing their depth and resonance.

0.4 The Role of Psychology in Interactive Narratives

Psychology plays a crucial role in shaping the creation and consumption of interactive narratives. It's a tool for understanding player behavior, for crafting narratives that captivate and engage, for designing choices that challenge and provoke. Moreover, it's a lens through which we can examine the psychological impact of interactive storytelling, from the thrill of agency to the immersion in a self-shaped narrative. In this section, we'll begin to uncover the psychological layers of interactive narratives, setting the stage for a deeper exploration in the chapters to come.

The psychology of player behavior is a fascinating aspect of interactive narratives. It allows creators to anticipate and understand how players might react to different scenarios, what motivates them, and how they derive enjoyment or satisfaction from the game. This knowledge influences the design of game mechanics, the structure of the narrative, and the overall user experience. By understanding the psychological underpinnings of player behavior, we can create interactive narratives that are not only engaging but also deeply resonant.

Beyond player behavior, the psychology of interactive narratives also encompasses the impact of these narratives on the players' minds. The sense of agency and immersion that interactive narratives provide can evoke powerful emotional responses, shape perceptions, and even influence decision-making processes. By delving into the psychological effects of interactive storytelling, we can understand its transformative potential, its capacity to influence not just in-game decisions, but real-world perspectives and actions.

In essence, psychology forms the backbone of interactive narratives, influencing their creation and their impact. As we navigate the enchanting labyrinth of adventure games and interactive storytelling, we'll continually explore these psychological aspects, enriching our understanding and appreciation of this innovative narrative form. This exploration will not only inform our discussion of the practical aspects of creating interactive narratives but also illuminate the profound ways in which these narratives engage, immerse, and transform players.

0.5   The Journey Ahead

Our journey into the labyrinthine world of interactive narratives is just beginning. In the chapters ahead, we'll delve deeper into the art and craft of creating adventure games, exploring everything from character development and dialogue writing to puzzle design and environmental storytelling. We'll also continue to delve into the philosophical and psychological layers of interactive narratives, uncovering the profound depths of this innovative storytelling medium. So, let's step forward, cross the threshold, and embark on this exciting adventure into the realm of interactive storytelling.

From understanding the history and evolution of adventure games to dissecting the anatomy of an interactive story, each chapter will unravel a new facet of this complex craft. We'll probe into the role of choice, consequence, and player agency, exploring how these elements shape the narrative and the player's experience. Moreover, we'll delve into the intricacies of designing puzzles and challenges, creating engaging characters and dialogues, and using the game environment as a narrative tool. Each chapter will not only provide practical guidance but also stimulate thought and inspire creativity.

In this journey, you are not just a passive reader but an active participant. You'll be invited to reflect on philosophical questions, analyze game design choices, and even apply the concepts learned by creating your own mini interactive narratives. By the end of this book, you should not only have a comprehensive understanding of creating interactive narratives but also have experienced the joy and challenges of this craft firsthand. So, are you ready to look door, get key, and unlock the captivating world of interactive storytelling? The adventure awaits.

Chapter 1: The Art of Adventure Games

The real voyage of discovery consists not in seeking new landscapes, but in having new eyes. - Marcel Proust

1.1   The Birth of Adventure Games

In a world before high-definition graphics and immersive virtual realities, adventure games were born. They emerged from the realms of text-based interactive fiction, where the players' imagination painted the world and the choices they made drove the story forward. This section will take you back to those early days, introducing you to the pioneers who dared to bring stories to life through the medium of games and set the stage for a genre that would captivate millions.

The first adventure games were simple, yet ground-breaking. They allowed players to interact with a virtual world in a way that was unprecedented at the time. These games, like 'Colossal Cave Adventure' and 'Zork', relied on text commands to navigate through a virtual world. The player's interaction with the game was through a parser, which took typed input and returned a textual response, creating a unique narrative for each player.

Despite their simplicity, these early games laid the groundwork for the future of the genre. They introduced concepts such as exploration, puzzle-solving, and player agency, which have become integral to adventure games. These pioneers proved that games could be more than just reflex-based challenges. They could be mediums for telling stories, for immersing players in worlds of the creators' imaginations, and for giving players the power to shape those stories through their choices.

1.2 Evolution of Adventure Games

Like all forms of art, adventure games have evolved over time, adapting to new technologies, changing player expectations, and the ever-expanding horizons of the gaming industry. This section will guide you through this evolution, tracing the journey of adventure games from their text-based origins to the captivating graphical narratives of today. As we chart this course, you'll come to understand how the genre has grown, innovated, and adapted while remaining true to its core principles.

The shift from text-based to graphical interfaces marked a significant turning point in the evolution of adventure games. As technology advanced, creators began to incorporate images and later, animations, adding a new layer of immersion to the gaming experience. This not only expanded the possibilities for storytelling but also opened up the genre to a wider audience, making adventure games more accessible and engaging for players of all ages.

As technology continued to evolve, so did the complexity of adventure games. The advent of 3D graphics and voice acting brought characters and worlds to life in ways previously unimaginable. Meanwhile, improvements in user interfaces and game mechanics allowed for more intricate puzzle designs and deeper narrative structures. Each technological advancement provided game designers with new tools to enhance player engagement and further push the boundaries of interactive storytelling.

Today, adventure games continue to evolve, embracing new technologies such as virtual and augmented reality, and exploring innovative narrative techniques like non-linear and branching storylines. The genre's ability to adapt and innovate, to harness the potential of new technologies in the service of storytelling, is a testament to its enduring appeal. As we look to the future, it is clear that adventure games will continue to captivate players, providing them with immersive narratives that are not just played, but experienced.

1.3   Impact on the Gaming Industry

The influence of adventure games extends beyond the boundaries of their own genre. They have left an indelible mark on the gaming industry as a whole, pushing narrative and character development to the forefront of game design. This section explores the ripple effect adventure games have created, dissecting their role in shaping the industry and influencing other genres.

The impact of adventure games is a testament to their importance and their enduring appeal.

Adventure games have played a crucial role in highlighting the importance of narrative within gaming. They demonstrated that games could be more than just mindless entertainment; they could be a medium for storytelling, just as compelling as any book or movie. This narrative focus has seeped into other genres, with RPGs, action-adventures, and even some first-person shooters incorporating strong story elements into their design. The rich, immersive narratives we see in many of today's games owe a debt to the pioneering work of adventure game developers.

The character development seen in adventure games has also had a significant influence. These games showed that players could form deep emotional connections with digital characters, driving home the idea that well-crafted characters could enhance player engagement and investment in the game. This emphasis on character has become a staple in many games today, across a variety of genres. It's a testament to the lasting impact of the adventure game genre.

1.4   Key Components of Adventure Games

Adventure games are a unique blend of various elements, each contributing to the overall experience in its own distinctive way. At their core, these games are about exploration. Players are dropped into a world filled with intrigue and mystery, and it's their task to uncover its secrets. This sense of exploration, of venturing into the unknown, is a fundamental component of adventure games.

Complementing the exploration is the challenge of puzzle-solving. Adventure games often present the player with a series of obstacles or puzzles that need to be overcome to progress. These puzzles can take many forms, from deciphering cryptic clues to manipulating the environment in creative ways. The satisfaction of solving these puzzles forms a crucial part of the player's engagement with the game.

However, what truly sets adventure games apart is their emphasis on narrative. Unlike many other genres, where the story often takes a backseat to gameplay, in adventure games, the narrative is front and center. The choices players make have tangible impacts on the story's progression, making them active participants in the unfolding drama. This strong narrative focus, combined with exploration and puzzle-solving, creates an immersive, engaging experience that defines the genre of adventure games.

1.5 Notable Adventure Games and Their Contributions

Throughout the history of adventure games, there have been titles that stood out, games that pushed the boundaries and in doing so, left a lasting impact on the genre and the industry. This section will spotlight some of these notable adventure games. Through their innovations, successes, and even their failures, we can glean insights into what makes an adventure game resonate with players and stand the test of time.

One of the earliest and most influential titles in the genre was 'Zork'. Released in the late 70s by Infocom, 'Zork' was a text-based game that thrived on challenging puzzles and richly detailed descriptions. It was a beacon of interactive storytelling, demonstrating the power of narrative and player choice in creating a captivating gaming experience.

Fast-forward to the 90s, and we witness the rise of 'Myst', a game that redefined the adventure genre with its stunning graphics, immersive world, and intricate puzzles. 'Myst' showed that adventure games could be visual masterpieces, seamlessly blending narrative and gameplay within beautifully crafted environments.

In the new millennium, games like 'Heavy Rain' and 'Life is Strange' further pushed the boundaries of the genre. They emphasized emotional storytelling, character development, and moral choices, proving that adventure games could be platforms for deep, mature narratives. These games, along with many others, have contributed to the evolution of the genre, each leaving their unique imprint and pushing the boundaries of what adventure games can be.

Chapter 2: The Anatomy of an Interactive Story

Stories are a communal currency of humanity. - Tahir Shah

2.1 Section 2.1: Understanding Interactive Narratives

In this section, we begin our exploration into the world of interactive narratives. Unlike traditional narratives which follow a linear path, interactive narratives offer a dynamic storytelling experience, allowing readers to influence the story's progression. They are not mere spectators but active participants in the unfolding of the narrative. Let's dive into the unique characteristics that define these narratives and set them apart from conventional storytelling.

Interactive narratives are often distinguished by their non-linearity. This means that the story does not follow a predetermined, straight path from start to finish. Instead, it branches off into multiple directions based on the choices made by the reader or player. This creates a unique narrative experience for each individual, as the story adjusts and changes according to their decisions.

However, the power of interactive narratives goes beyond their non-linearity. These narratives also offer a sense of agency, allowing the reader or player to feel like they have a direct impact on the story's outcome. This sense of agency is crucial in creating a more immersive and engaging narrative experience. By giving readers the power to influence the narrative, interactive stories transform passive readers into active participants, creating a deeper emotional connection to the story.

2.2 Section 2.2: The Structure of Interactive Stories

The structure of interactive stories is a curious labyrinth, a complex web of interwoven paths and possibilities. Unlike linear narratives which have a clear beginning, middle, and end, interactive stories present a multi-faceted narrative structure. They offer multiple beginnings, middles, and endings, all shaped by the choices the player makes. Hence, the narrative structure transforms into a dynamic entity, constantly evolving with each player's decisions.

This complex structure, often visualized as a tree diagram, is known as branching narrative. Each branch represents a path the narrative could take, and each node or point on the branch represents a choice point. Choice points are critical moments in the narrative where the player must make a decision, and these decisions determine the direction of the story. The challenge for the writer, then, is to manage these branching narratives in a way that maintains story coherence and player engagement.

To create a compelling interactive narrative, the writer must consider the balance between player choice and story coherence. Although it's essential to provide players with meaningful choices, these choices must also lead to satisfying narrative outcomes. This often involves creating a balance between branching paths (divergent storytelling) and merging paths (convergent storytelling). While divergent storytelling offers a breadth of narrative possibilities, convergent storytelling ensures the story remains manageable and coherent regardless of the choices made.

2.3 Section 2.3: Choice Points and Branching Narratives

At the heart of interactive storytelling lie choice points and branching narratives. These elements give players the freedom to shape their narrative journey, transforming them from passive consumers into active contributors. But how can we create choices that are meaningful and branches that diverge and converge in a way that maintains narrative coherence? This section will unravel the art and science behind designing engaging choice points and managing branching narratives.

Choice points are critical moments in the narrative where a decision needs to be made. They can be as simple as choosing which path to take in a forest or as complex as deciding whether to trust a mysterious character. These choices should be meaningful and have consequences, affecting the story's progression and outcome. Designing impactful choice points involves a deep understanding of your characters, your narrative, and your players.

Branching narratives, on the other hand, are the different paths that the story can take based on the player's choices. The challenge here is creating a multitude of narrative branches that are unique and engaging, yet converge in a way that maintains the story's coherence and integrity. It's like weaving a tapestry where each thread is a narrative branch, and the resulting pattern is a coherent, engaging story.

However, creating meaningful choice points and managing branching narratives is not an easy task. It requires careful planning, creativity, and a solid understanding of narrative design. But the rewards are well worth the effort. Through well-designed choice points and carefully managed branching narratives, you can create a rich, interactive narrative that resonates with your players and leaves a lasting impact.

2.4 Section 2.4: Creating Immersive Interactive Experiences

Crafting an interactive narrative goes beyond designing choices and branches—it's about creating a deeply immersive experience. This involves giving the player a sense of agency, stirring their emotions, and maintaining a gripping narrative pace. But how do we achieve these elements in an interactive story? In this section, we will delve into strategies for creating immersive experiences that captivate players and keep them hooked on the narrative journey.

Player agency, the feeling that the player's actions have a meaningful impact on the story's outcome, is a crucial aspect of immersion. When players feel that their decisions matter, they invest emotionally in the story, leading to a more engaging and satisfying experience. To foster this sense of agency, choices presented to the player must carry weight—consequences should be significant, and the narrative should reflect the player's decisions in meaningful ways.

Emotional engagement is another vital factor in creating immersive interactive experiences. This is achieved by crafting compelling characters, relatable conflicts, and evocative settings. By making players care about the characters and the world they inhabit, we can motivate them to engage actively with the narrative. Emotional engagement can also be enhanced by incorporating elements of surprise, suspense, and moral dilemmas into the story.

Narrative pacing—how the story unfolds over time—is also essential in maintaining player immersion. Too slow, and the player may lose interest; too fast, and the player may feel overwhelmed. It is crucial to strike the right balance, ensuring the narrative progresses at a pace that keeps the player engaged without sacrificing depth and complexity. This involves careful planning of plot points, choice moments, and narrative branches.

In conclusion, creating immersive interactive experiences is no mean feat—it involves a delicate balance of player agency, emotional engagement, and narrative pacing. However, with careful planning and thoughtful design, it is possible to craft interactive narratives that captivate players and provide a deeply satisfying and immersive experience. Remember, in the world of interactive storytelling, the player is not just a reader, but a co-author—and your role is to provide them with the tools and opportunities to write a story that is uniquely theirs.

2.5 Section 2.5: Tools for Building Interactive Narratives

Creating interactive narratives can seem like a daunting task, but with the right tools and frameworks, it becomes a manageable and highly rewarding process. This section introduces a selection of tools designed to aid in the creation of interactive stories, from concept to execution. These tools can provide a solid foundation for budding game designers and writers, enabling them to bring their interactive narratives to life.

One of the most popular tools for creating interactive narratives is Twine. Twine is an open-source tool that allows writers to create interactive stories in the form of web pages. It has a visual interface that makes it easy to design branching narratives and implement player choices. It's a great tool for beginners, as it requires no coding knowledge but still offers a lot of flexibility for more advanced users.

Ink by Inkle Studios is another excellent tool for writing interactive narratives. It is more text-focused and is excellent for crafting complex, branching stories with a lot of narrative depth. Ink also integrates well with Unity, a popular game development platform, making it a favorite among game developers. But no matter which tool you choose, remember that the most important thing is your story. The tool is just there to help you bring it to life.

Finally, it's worth mentioning platforms like ChoiceScript and Adventure Game Studio. ChoiceScript is a simple scripting language developed by Choice of Games for writing multiple-choice games. Adventure Game Studio, on the other hand, is perfect for those looking to create graphical adventure games. Each tool has its strengths and would suit different kinds of interactive stories.

In conclusion, while the task of creating interactive narratives may initially seem daunting, the right tools can make the process manageable and rewarding. The tools mentioned in this section are just a few examples of what's available. As you delve deeper into interactive storytelling, you may find other tools that better suit your style and needs. Remember, the tool is only as good as the story it helps create. So focus on your narrative, and let the tools help you bring it to life.

Chapter 3: Choice, Consequence, and Agency

Life is a matter of choices, and every choice you make makes you. - John C. Maxwell

3.1 Understanding Player Choice

As we venture into the heart of interactive storytelling, the concept of player choice emerges as a pivotal element. From the simplest decision of which path to take, to the weighty moral dilemmas that can alter the course of the narrative, choices are the essence of adventure games. In this first section, we will delve into the myriad forms of player choice, examining how each one impacts the gaming experience and shapes the unfolding story.

Player choice in adventure games is not always as straightforward as it seems. Choices can range from explicit options presented to the player, to implicit decisions made through gameplay actions. An explicit choice could be a dialogue option that directly influences the character's relationships and the narrative direction. Implicit choices, on the other hand, could be as subtle as choosing which areas to explore first, implicitly shaping the player's experience and understanding of the game world.

The power of choice also lies in its ability to personalize the gaming experience. Each player's unique combination of choices leads to a distinct narrative journey, creating a storyline that is uniquely their own. This personalized narrative is one of the fundamental appeals of adventure games, offering an immersive experience that is tailored to each player's decisions. In the following sections, we will explore how these choices lead to consequences and create a sense of agency, shaping the heart and soul of adventure gaming.

3.2 Consequences in Gameplay

Every choice has a consequence. This is a universal truth, resounding loud and clear in the realm of adventure games. As the player navigates through the narrative labyrinth, each decision leads to a ripple of outcomes, affecting both the game world and the storyline. This section will explore the intricate web of consequences that stems from player choices, and how these outcomes can enrich the gameplay and narrative.

In the context of adventure games, consequences are not merely the result of choices; they are the bridge that connects the player's decisions to the narrative. They are the tangible evidence of the impact of the player's choices. Whether it's a dialogue option that alters a character's perception, a path chosen that reveals a new environment, or a puzzle solved that advances the story, each consequence is a reflection of the player's agency in the gaming world.

However, designing meaningful consequences is no small task. It involves careful planning, intricate narrative design, and a deep understanding of player psychology. Developers must ensure that the consequences feel natural and logical while also being surprising and impactful. Additionally, they must consider the long-term effects of these consequences on the game's narrative, ensuring that each choice leads to satisfying and coherent outcomes.

In essence, consequences are the lifeblood of interactive storytelling in adventure games. They give weight to the player's choices, shape the narrative, and provide the tension and unpredictability that make the gaming experience so compelling. As we delve deeper into the world of interactive storytelling, understanding the role and design of consequences becomes paramount in crafting engaging and immersive adventure games.

3.3 Creating a Sense of Agency

Agency—the sense that a player's actions have meaningful impact—is a cornerstone of compelling interactive storytelling. It's not enough for players to merely choose; they must feel that their decisions carry weight in the game world, influencing characters, events, and the narrative itself. In this section, we will discuss how the interplay of choice and consequence fosters a sense of agency, deepening player engagement and immersion.

When players perceive that their decisions have real, tangible effects, they become more invested in the game. They start to care about the characters and the world they inhabit, and they become more engaged in the unfolding narrative. The sense of agency can be a powerful tool for creating emotional resonance, as players feel a personal stake in the outcomes of their actions. This can lead to more immersive and memorable gaming experiences.

However, creating a sense of agency is not without its challenges. It requires careful narrative design and thoughtful consideration of player choices and their outcomes. The consequences must be clear and meaningful, and the choices must be varied and significant. But when done right, the sense of agency can transform a game from a passive experience into an active, engaging journey.

3.4 Balancing Choices and Consequences

Creating a game where every choice leads to a unique outcome sounds enticing, but it can quickly devolve into narrative chaos. Striking a balance between offering meaningful choices and managing their consequences is a delicate art—one that we will explore in this section. We will discuss strategies to maintain this equilibrium, ensuring that the game remains cohesive, engaging, and manageable, even as it branches into myriad possibilities.

The first strategy involves limiting the magnitude of the consequences. Not every choice needs to dramatically alter the narrative. Some decisions can have subtler effects, influencing character interactions or revealing new aspects of the story. These smaller consequences can still foster a sense of agency without derailing the main narrative. On the other hand, major choices that significantly impact the game world should be used sparingly and with careful consideration, to avoid overwhelming the player and diluting the impact of these moments.

The second strategy revolves around the use of converging paths. While each choice may initially lead the player down different narrative branches, these branches can eventually converge back to key plot points. This approach, known as the 'illusion of choice', maintains narrative cohesion and control, while still offering players the satisfaction of shaping their own journey.

Lastly, there's the strategy of managing player expectations. From the outset, it's important to communicate to the players the kind of game they're playing. Is it a game where every decision could have far-reaching consequences, or a game where the narrative is largely predetermined with choices serving to personalize the experience? Setting clear expectations can help players understand and accept the level of impact their choices will have on the game's narrative.

Balancing choices and consequences can be a challenging task, but it is central to creating a fulfilling and engaging adventure game. By keeping these strategies in mind and applying them judiciously, game designers can craft interactive narratives that are rich with meaningful choices, without descending into chaos.

3.5 Case Studies of Choice and Consequence

Theory and practice often diverge, and it is in the crucible of real games that the concepts of choice, consequence, and agency are truly tested. This section will examine case studies of adventure games that have effectively harnessed these elements to enhance player engagement. Through these examples, we will gain insight into the practical application of the concepts we've discussed and glean inspiration for our own interactive narratives.

Let's begin with one of the most renowned examples in the genre—Telltale Games' The Walking Dead. This game masterfully intertwines player choice and consequence, with decisions not only affecting the narrative progression but also the relationships between characters. The emotional weight carried by these choices enhances player engagement, making The Walking Dead a compelling interactive experience.

Another noteworthy example is Quantic Dream's Heavy Rain, a game that pushes the envelope of interactive storytelling with its 'butterfly effect' narrative. Every choice, no matter how small, can lead to a cascade of consequences, creating a vast array of narrative pathways. This level of complexity and unpredictability keeps players invested in the story, reinforcing the notion that their actions truly matter.

Finally, we turn to BioWare's Mass Effect series, celebrated for its deep character interactions and branching narrative. Players' choices not only shape the course of the story but also the development of their character and relationships. The series' commitment to consequential storytelling fosters a strong sense of agency, making each playthrough a unique, personal experience.

3.6   The Ethical Dimensions of Choice

The power of choice carries with it an ethical dimension. Adventure games often present players with moral dilemmas, using the interactive medium to provoke thought and stir emotions. In this final section, we will explore how the ethical implications of choice can be used to deliver powerful messages, elevate the narrative, and create a deeper, more thought-provoking gaming experience.

Choices in adventure games are not always about strategy or solving puzzles; sometimes, they are about morality and ethics. These choices challenge players, forcing them to grapple with tough decisions that have no clear right or wrong answers. This is where adventure games truly shine, using their interactive nature to engage players on a deeply personal level and make them ponder over their decisions.

To illustrate this, let's consider a game where the player, as a leader of a struggling post-apocalyptic community, has to decide who gets the last piece of food. The choice isn't just about who lives and who dies—it's about the values of the community, the weight of leadership, and the harsh realities of survival. This moral quandary engages players on an emotional level, making the experience more immersive and impactful.

In conclusion, the ethical dimensions of choice in adventure games open up avenues for deep, thoughtful narratives. By incorporating moral and ethical dilemmas into gameplay, developers can create experiences

that resonate with players on a personal level. The
choices we make in games, like the choices we make in
life, shape us—and in the hands of a skilled developer,
they can shape powerful, unforgettable narratives.

Chapter 4: Designing Puzzles and Challenges

Every problem is a gift without problems we would not grow. - Anthony Robbins

4.1   Understanding the Role of Puzzles

The role of puzzles in adventure games is akin to the heart within the human body. They pump vital engagement and challenge into the game, keeping the player immersed and invested. In this section, we'll explore the importance and impact of puzzles, shedding light on how they contribute to the overall gaming experience and why they are often considered the lifeblood of adventure games.

Every puzzle in an adventure game serves a dual purpose: it presents a challenge to the player, and it propels the story forward. A well-crafted puzzle is not only satisfying to solve but also furthers the game's narrative, adding a layer of depth to the story. It engages the player's intellect, stimulates their curiosity, and rewards them with the joy of discovery and progression upon its successful resolution.

However, creating effective puzzles is not without its challenges. It requires a keen understanding of player psychology, a knack for suspense and timing, and a deep respect for the game's narrative. The puzzle must be balanced in difficulty, not too easy to solve that it feels inconsequential, and not too hard that it becomes a roadblock. It must feel integral to the game world and the story, seamlessly blending with the narrative threads and the game's environment.

4.2   Types of Puzzles

Just as there are myriad types of adventure games, so too are there a plethora of puzzles. Each type serves a different purpose, adds a unique flavor to the gameplay, and offers a distinct challenge to the player. In this section, we'll journey through various types of puzzles, offering examples and discussing how they can be effectively incorporated into your game to enrich the player's experience.

One of the most common types of puzzles in adventure games is the 'lock and key' puzzle. This involves finding an item (the 'key') and using it to unlock a new area or gain access to a crucial object (the 'lock'). The key could be a literal key, a code, a password, or any object that, when used correctly, progresses the game. These puzzles are straightforward and easy to understand, making them a staple in many adventure games.

Another type of puzzle is the 'riddle' or 'clue' puzzle. This involves the player receiving a riddle or clue that they must solve to progress. The solution could lead to a location, reveal a hidden item, or uncover a critical piece of the game's story. These puzzles require players to think more deeply and can add a layer of mystery and intrigue to your game.

The 'environmental' puzzle utilizes the game's environment as a part of the puzzle itself. Players might need to manipulate their surroundings, like moving objects, triggering mechanisms, or observing patterns in the environment to solve the puzzle. These puzzles can be particularly immersive, drawing players deeper into the game world.

Finally, there are 'logic' puzzles. These puzzles require players to use logical thinking to solve a problem or sequence. This could involve solving a mathematical problem, deciphering a code, or figuring out a sequence of events. These puzzles can offer a satisfying challenge for players who enjoy mental exercises.

Each type of puzzle brings its own unique charm to an adventure game. The key is to understand your target audience and the type of challenges they would enjoy. By incorporating a variety of puzzles, you can ensure your game offers a diverse and engaging experience that caters to a wide range of players.

4.3   Designing Engaging Puzzles

Designing a puzzle is an art form, one that requires a delicate balance of creativity, logic, and a deep understanding of the player's mindset. An engaging puzzle can elevate an adventure game from good to unforgettable. In this section, we'll delve into the principles and guidelines for designing puzzles that are not just challenging, but also captivating, keeping players hooked and eager for more.

The first step in designing an engaging puzzle is understanding your player's mindset. What are their expectations? What level of complexity can they handle? What kind of challenges do they enjoy? These questions should be at the heart of your puzzle design process. It's essential to create puzzles that match your target audience's skill level and taste, as this will ensure they remain engaged and invested in the gameplay.

Next, your puzzles should serve a purpose within the game's narrative. They shouldn't be random obstacles, but meaningful challenges that push the story forward. Whether it's unlocking a door to reveal a new area, deciphering a code to access crucial information, or overcoming a trap to progress, each puzzle should have a clear connection to the story and the game world.

Lastly, remember that the best puzzles are those that encourage players to think outside the box. They should challenge the player's problem-solving skills, forcing them to think creatively and strategically. However, it's important to ensure the solution is always fair and logical within the game's context. There's nothing more frustrating for a player than a puzzle that seems unsolvable or a solution that feels random and disconnected from the rest of the game.

4.4 Balancing Difficulty and Accessibility

Creating a puzzle that's too easy can lead to disinterest and disengagement from players, while one that's too difficult can lead to frustration and a potential disconnection from the game. Striking the right balance between difficulty and accessibility is not just an art, but a crucial aspect of maintaining player engagement and enjoyment. This balance ensures that your puzzles not only challenge players but also keep them invested in the game. The key is to create puzzles that are just challenging enough to provoke thought and stimulate a sense of accomplishment upon solving them.

Balancing difficulty and accessibility can be achieved through various strategies. One effective method is implementing a tiered difficulty system, where puzzles progressively get harder as players advance through the game. This allows players to gradually build up their problem-solving skills and confidence. Another strategy is to provide subtle hints or clues within the game environment or dialogue, aiding players when they are stuck without explicitly giving away the solution. These hints can be cleverly woven into the narrative, further enhancing the game's immersive quality.

Accessibility also extends to the user interface and

controls used to solve puzzles. It's important to ensure that the mechanics of interacting with puzzles are intuitive and user-friendly. Players should be able to focus on solving the puzzle itself, not struggling with how to input their solutions. Furthermore, consider incorporating options for players with different abilities, such as colorblind modes or alternate control schemes, to make your game inclusive and accessible to all. In the next section, we will delve into how puzzles can be seamlessly integrated into the game's narrative, enhancing the story and the player's immersion.

4.5   Puzzles and Narrative Integration

Puzzles in an adventure game should not be an afterthought or a mere obstacle for the player to overcome. Instead, they should be intricately woven into the storyline, becoming a part of the narrative tapestry. This integration not only enhances the narrative but also ups the ante for the player, making the puzzles more than just brain teasers. They become meaningful pieces of the story, driving the narrative forward.

To achieve this, the puzzle design process should begin with the narrative. Consider the story you're telling, the setting, the characters, and the overarching themes. How can puzzles be used to deepen the player's understanding of these elements? How can they be used to reveal character motivations or plot twists? When you start by considering the narrative, the puzzles naturally become a part of the story, rather than feeling tacked on or out of place.

However, integrating puzzles into the narrative isn't just about making them fit within the story. It's also about using them to enhance the player's immersion. A well-designed, narrative-integrated puzzle can make the player feel more connected to the game world and more invested in the story. It can make the difference between a player simply playing a game and a player being truly engaged in an interactive narrative experience. In the following sections, we'll explore specific techniques and examples of how to achieve this seamless puzzle-narrative integration.

Chapter 5: Writing Characters and Dialogues

Character is like a tree and reputation like a shadow. - Abraham Lincoln

5.1 Understanding Character Roles in Adventure Games

As we venture into the heart of any narrative, it's the characters that breathe life into the story. In adventure games, they become the vehicles through which players navigate, explore, and understand the game world. This section will delve into the critical roles characters play in adventure games, from protagonists to supporting characters, and how they drive the narrative forward. A clear understanding of these roles is essential in creating an engaging and immersive gaming experience.

In an adventure game, the protagonist serves as the player's avatar, their conduit into the game world. The protagonist's actions, decisions, and experiences are those of the player, creating a profound connection that can make the game an emotionally engaging experience. The protagonist's personality, backstory, motivations, and evolution are crucial elements that need meticulous crafting. This character's journey forms the backbone of the game's narrative, making them central to the player's experience.

Supporting characters, on the other hand, enrich the game world and contribute to the narrative in various ways. They can provide information, aid or hinder the protagonist, and add depth to the story. Supporting characters can include allies, antagonists, and neutral characters who inhabit the game world. Each of these characters has a role to play in the narrative and the player's experience. Their personalities, backstories, and motivations should be just as carefully crafted as those of the protagonist.

In creating characters for adventure games, it's also

crucial to consider the roles they play in terms of game mechanics. Characters can be quest givers, gatekeepers, or sources of aid or hindrance to the player. The characters' roles in the game mechanics should align with their roles in the narrative to create a cohesive and immersive experience. Understanding these roles and how to leverage them effectively is a key part of writing characters for adventure games.

5.2   Crafting Compelling Characters

Creating compelling characters is an art. These characters must resonate with players, evoking a range of emotions and facilitating a deep connection with the game's narrative. This section will guide you through the process of crafting engaging and relatable characters, taking into account various aspects such as backstory, motivation, and character arcs. By mastering these elements, you can create characters that leave a lasting impact on your players.

A character's backstory is not just their history; it's the foundation upon which their personality is built. It provides context to their actions, attitudes, and motivations within the game. When designing a character's backstory, consider their upbringing, past experiences, relationships, and major life events. Each of these elements contributes to shaping the character's personality, beliefs, and goals, making them feel more real and relatable to players.

Motivation is the driving force behind a character's actions. It gives purpose to their journey and guides their decisions throughout the game. When crafting character motivations, consider what they desire, fear, or value. These motivations should be deeply tied to the game's narrative, pushing the character—and thus the player—forward. Remember, a character's motivation can evolve as the story progresses, reflecting their growth and development.

Finally, a character's arc is their journey of change and evolution throughout the game. It's the transformation they undergo as they face challenges, overcome obstacles, and make difficult choices. A well-crafted character arc can make a character more dynamic and engaging, providing a satisfying narrative experience for the player. Whether a character emerges victorious, finds redemption, or succumbs to their flaws, their arc should be meaningful and impactful, leaving a lasting impression on the player.

5.3 Writing Dynamic Dialogues

Dialogue in adventure games serves multiple functions. It is the primary medium through which characters express their personalities, thoughts, and emotions. This makes it an invaluable tool for revealing who a character is beyond their visual design. Each line of dialogue should be crafted with the character's personality, history, and motivations in mind, providing subtle hints about their character traits and backstory.

Beyond character revelation, dialogue is instrumental in advancing the plot. It can be used to present new information, create conflict, and resolve tension. Effective dialogue can keep players engaged, driving the narrative forward in a dynamic and intriguing manner. However, it's essential to avoid 'information dumps' where characters unrealistically divulge important information, instead, strive for a natural progression of dialogue that seamlessly integrates with the plot.

Dialogue also plays a crucial role in providing players with necessary information. It can be used to guide players, offer hints, or reveal important aspects of the game world. This, however, should be done subtly to avoid breaking the immersion. Remember, players don't want to feel like they're being spoon-fed information. Instead, they should feel like they're uncovering it themselves as a part of their adventure.

5.4   Balancing Dialogue and Gameplay

In an adventure game, dialogue and gameplay must exist in harmony. While dialogue is crucial for character development and plot progression, it must not hinder the gameplay or overwhelm the player. This delicate balance is critical in maintaining player engagement and immersion. As such, understanding how to strike this balance is a key skill for any adventure game writer.

Dialogue can enhance gameplay by providing context, revealing character motivations, or hinting at possible solutions to puzzles. However, it's important to avoid lengthy dialogues that disrupt the game's pacing or become tedious. Instead, aim to use succinct and purposeful dialogue that enhances the player's understanding and enjoyment of the game. Remember, every line of dialogue should serve a purpose, whether it's to advance the plot, develop a character, or provide clues for the player.

Achieving balance also involves considering the player's control over dialogue choices. In many adventure games, players can choose their responses during conversations, which can impact the narrative and game-play. Offering meaningful dialogue choices can enhance player engagement, but it's crucial not to overwhelm the player with too many options or insignificant choices. The key is to provide choices that feel significant and have clear, understandable consequences, furthering the interactivity and immersive quality of the game.

5.5   Using Characters and Dialogues to Shape Player Choices

Characters and dialogues don't just shape the narrative; they also shape player choices. The way a character speaks, acts, and reacts can influence a player's decisions and, consequently, the direction of the narrative. This section will discuss how to use characters and dialogues effectively to guide player choices and shape the narrative in the realm of interactive storytelling.

Every choice a player makes in an adventure game is often a direct response to a character's actions or words. For instance, a player might decide to trust a character based on their honest and open dialogue, or choose to explore a particular path because a character hinted at something interesting in that direction. Therefore, as a game writer, it's crucial to understand the power your characters and their dialogues wield in shaping a player's journey through the game.

But how do you ensure your characters and dialogues effectively shape player choices? The key lies in authenticity and consistent characterization. Players should feel that the choices they are making are authentic responses to the situation at hand, not forced or arbitrary. Similarly, characters must react consistently to player choices, reinforcing the believable and dynamic nature of the game world. When these elements are skillfully combined, they can profoundly influence player choices, creating a deeply engaging and interactive narrative experience.

In the end, characters and dialogues are not just tools to tell a story; they are also tools to guide player choices. They provide the framework within which players can make meaningful decisions, impacting the narrative's direction and outcome. By mastering the art of character and dialogue writing, you can create a rich and interactive narrative that responds to and evolves with the player's choices, providing a truly immersive adventure gaming experience.

5.6 Case Studies - Effective Characters and Dialogues in Popular Adventure Games

Learning from successful examples is one of the best ways to improve your craft. In this section, we'll look at case studies of effective character creation and dialogue writing in popular adventure games. These practical examples will provide valuable insights and inspiration, helping you understand how to apply the principles and techniques discussed in this chapter to your own game narratives.

Our first case study is the iconic adventure game, 'The Secret of Monkey Island.' This game is renowned for its memorable characters and witty dialogues. The protagonist, Guybrush Threepwood, is a relatable underdog whose humorous dialogues and quirky personality make him an unforgettable character. His interactions with the other characters, especially the villainous LeChuck, are filled with humor and clever wordplay, demonstrating the effective use of dialogue to reveal character personalities and advance the narrative.

Next, we turn to the critically acclaimed 'Life is Strange.' This episodic adventure game is a masterclass in character development and dialogue writing. The game's protagonist, Max Caulfield, is a high school student with the ability to rewind time. Her dialogues, internal monologues, and interactions with other characters reveal her personality, her struggles, and her growth throughout the game. The game also effectively uses dialogue to foreshadow events, build tension, and influence player choices, demonstrating the power of well-crafted dialogue in shaping the narrative and the player's experience.

Lastly, let's consider 'The Walking Dead' game series by Telltale Games. This game is famous for its deep, complex characters and the impactful choices that players must make. The dialogues in this game are not only used to reveal character personalities and advance the plot, but also to present players with difficult moral dilemmas. The choices players make in dialogues significantly affect the narrative and the fate of the characters, illustrating the critical role of dialogue in interactive storytelling.

These case studies highlight the importance of effective character creation and dialogue writing in adventure games. They serve as practical examples of how to apply the principles and techniques discussed in this chapter. By studying these examples and understanding the strategies used, you can enhance your ability to create engaging characters and dialogues in your own adventure games. Remember, characters and dialogues are not just elements of your game – they are the heart and soul of your narrative.

Chapter 6: The Role of Environment in Storytelling

Environment is the invisible hand that
shapes human behavior. - James Clear

6.1 The Language of Game Environments

In the realm of adventure games, environments are not just backdrops—they are characters in their own right. As we begin this exploration into the language of game environments, we'll see how they communicate vital elements of the narrative, lending depth and complexity without uttering a single word. This silent storytelling, achieved through careful design and placement of visual elements, allows players to uncover the narrative organically, enhancing their engagement and immersion in the game world.

Game environments speak a visual language, telling stories through every pixel. From the ancient ruins hinting at a fallen civilization to the ominous, shadowy corridors foretelling danger, each element is a narrative beat, a piece of the puzzle that players piece together as they explore. This environmental storytelling is intrinsic to the adventure game genre, fostering a deep sense of discovery and curiosity, and rewarding observant players with richer narrative experiences.

The silent dialogue between the player and the game environment is a delicate dance of show and tell. The environment shows, hinting at past events, setting the mood, and hinting at future possibilities. Meanwhile, the player, driven by their curiosity, tells by choosing where to go, what to investigate, and how to interpret the signs and symbols within the environment. In this way, the game environment becomes an active participant in the storytelling, shaping the player's understanding and experience of the narrative.

6.2 Crafting Immersive Worlds

Creating a world that captivates players and serves the game's narrative is an art form. In this section, we delve into the techniques and strategies that breathe life into game environments, from the grandest landscapes to the smallest details. We'll explore how to craft immersive worlds that not only entice players to explore but also deepen their connection to the narrative, making every action feel meaningful and consequential.

The first step in creating a compelling game environment is world-building. This involves creating a detailed and consistent setting for your game, complete with its own history, culture, and rules. This foundational work not only gives your game a sense of authenticity but also provides a rich tapestry on which to weave your narrative. By embedding the story within the very fabric of the game world, you enhance the player's sense of immersion and engagement.

Interactive elements are another crucial component of an immersive game environment. By allowing players to interact with their surroundings in meaningful ways, you give them a sense of agency and influence over the game world. These interactions can range from simple actions like picking up objects to complex mechanics like affecting the weather or manipulating the environment to solve puzzles. By making the environment responsive to the player's actions, you can create a deeper sense of immersion and make the narrative feel more dynamic and engaging.

Finally, the aesthetic design of the game environment plays a significant role in crafting an immersive world. The visual style of the environment can evoke specific moods and emotions, enhancing the thematic depth of the narrative. Elements such as lighting, color palette, and architectural style can all be used to convey a certain atmosphere, further immersing players in the game world. By carefully considering these visual elements, you can create an environment that not only looks stunning but also serves the narrative and enhances the player's emotional connection to the game.

6.3   The Role of Environmental Puzzles

Puzzles are integral to adventure games, and when woven into the environment, they can propel the narrative in intriguing ways. In this section, we'll explore how environmental puzzles can be designed and integrated into the game world to advance the story. We'll look at examples from renowned adventure games, examining how their environmental puzzles not only challenge players but also reveal narrative threads that enrich the overall storytelling.

Environmental puzzles can be as simple as finding a hidden object or as complex as deciphering a series of cryptic symbols etched onto ancient walls. What sets them apart is their seamless integration into the game world. They don't stand out as puzzles to be solved but are part of the environment itself, requiring players to interact with their surroundings in creative and meaningful ways.

The most effective environmental puzzles are those that intertwine with the game's narrative. This means that solving them not only allows players to progress in the game but also uncovers new aspects of the story. This could be a revelation about a character's past, a clue to a looming threat, or a piece of the larger mystery that the game revolves around. Thus, these puzzles serve as narrative gateways, drawing players deeper into the game world.

6.4 Setting Mood and Tone through Environment

The environment in an adventure game is more than just a stage for the characters to move around in—it's a powerful narrative device that can evoke a spectrum of emotions and set the tone for the entire game. From the eerie, deserted streets of Silent Hill to the vibrant, bustling markets of Assassin's Creed, game environments can generate feelings of fear, excitement, curiosity, and more. They can transport players to different times and places, immersing them in worlds that feel real and alive. This section explores how game designers use environments to create emotional landscapes, influencing player responses and subtly guiding them through the narrative journey.

One way game designers create mood and tone is through the careful use of color and lighting. Much like in film and photography, these elements can significantly impact the atmosphere of a scene. Dark, desaturated colors and low, dramatic lighting can create a sense of foreboding, while bright, saturated colors and soft, even lighting can evoke feelings of joy and tranquility. By manipulating these elements, designers can guide players' emotional responses and shape their experiences in the game world.

Sound is another powerful tool for setting mood and tone. Ambient sounds like wind, rain, or distant chatter can make a game world feel more realistic and immersive. Meanwhile, music can dramatically enhance the emotional impact of a scene—think of the tense, high-tempo tracks that play during action sequences, or the soft, melancholic melodies that accompany more poignant moments. Sound and music, combined with visual elements, can create a rich, multi-sensory experience that deeply engages players and pulls them further into the game's narrative.

6.5   The Impact of Technological Advancements on Environmental Storytelling

The advent of new technologies has opened up unprecedented possibilities for environmental storytelling in adventure games. From the immersive landscapes of virtual reality to the blended realities of augmented reality, these advancements have enriched the narrative potential of game environments. In this section, we'll explore how these technologies have revolutionized environmental storytelling, offering game designers new ways to engage players and deepen their immersion in the narrative world.

Virtual reality (VR) has been at the forefront of this technological revolution. With the ability to create immersive, 360-degree environments, VR allows players to step directly into the game world. This level of immersion heightens the impact of environmental storytelling, as players can fully engage with the surroundings, exploring every nook and cranny, and experiencing the narrative in a deeply personal way.

Augmented reality (AR) offers another exciting avenue for environmental storytelling. By blending the real and virtual worlds, AR games can layer narrative elements onto our everyday environment, creating a unique form of storytelling that blurs the line between fiction and reality. This can lead to powerful narrative experiences, as the game world intersects with the player's personal environment, making the story feel more immediate and real.

Looking ahead, the continued advancement of these technologies promises to further enhance the power of environmental storytelling in adventure games. As game designers continue to experiment with these tools, we will undoubtedly see new forms of narrative emerge, pushing the boundaries of what is possible in interactive storytelling. The future of environmental storytelling is truly exciting, and we are just beginning to scratch the surface of its potential.

Chapter 7: Balancing Player Freedom and Narrative

Freedom is nothing but a chance to be better.
- Albert Camus

7.1 The Paradox of Choice

In the realm of adventure gaming, choice is often touted as a symbol of player freedom. The ability to explore, interact, and make decisions in the game world is seen as a cornerstone of the genre. Yet, the paradox of choice presents a unique challenge. When players are presented with too many options, the freedom that was meant to be empowering can become overwhelming.

This phenomenon, known as decision paralysis, is not exclusive to gaming. It's a psychological state where the pressure of making a decision becomes so overwhelming that the individual is rendered unable to make a choice at all. In the context of adventure games, this could lead to players disengaging from the game, finding the multitude of options more stressful than enjoyable.

Therefore, it's crucial for game designers to strike a balance. While player autonomy is important, it's equally essential to ensure that this freedom doesn't become a burden. By carefully curating the choices available and guiding players subtly, designers can create a sense of freedom without overwhelming them. In the following sections, we will delve deeper into how this balance can be achieved.

7.2   The Role of Constraints

The concept of freedom in gaming often conjures images of boundless landscapes waiting to be explored, limitless possibilities, and an array of choices for the players to make. However, in the world of interactive storytelling, total freedom can sometimes be a hindrance rather than a boon. It may seem counterintuitive, but constraints can often enhance a player's gaming experience by providing a structure within which they can make meaningful choices.

Constraints can come in many forms - limitations on time, resources, available actions, or even character abilities. These limitations can provide a framework for the narrative, guiding the story in a certain direction while still leaving room for player agency. The trick lies in implementing these constraints in a way that feels organic and integral to the game world, rather than arbitrary or restrictive.

For example, consider a game where the protagonist has a limited amount of time to accomplish a mission. This time constraint adds a sense of urgency and tension to the gameplay, pushing the player to make quick decisions and prioritize their actions. It also lends a degree of realism to the game, as real-world tasks often come with their own time constraints. Such constraints not only enrich the gameplay but also drive the narrative forward, ensuring a balance between player freedom and a coherent storyline.

7.3   Navigating the Narrative Landscape

The term 'open world' has become synonymous with player freedom in the gaming industry. Games that boast sprawling, explorable environments promise players an unparalleled sense of autonomy. However, crafting such expansive game worlds comes with its own set of challenges. The primary one being - how do you ensure that your player, who has the liberty to go anywhere and do anything, still ends up experiencing the key narrative moments that you've carefully designed?

The answer lies in the artful placement of narrative breadcrumbs. These are subtle clues and hints placed within the game environment that guide the player towards the main narrative. These could be visual cues, character dialogues, or even gameplay mechanics. The trick is to make these breadcrumbs compelling enough to entice the player, yet not so overt that they feel their hand is being held.

It's also crucial to design your game world in a way that naturally funnels players towards the narrative. This doesn't mean restricting their freedom, but rather subtly influencing their choices. Landmarks, environmental hazards, and even NPC (Non-Player Character) behaviors can all be used to gently nudge the player in the right direction. Remember, the goal is not to control the player, but to create an engaging narrative that they would want to follow.

7.4 Maintaining Narrative Coherence

As we venture further into the realm of interactive storytelling, a key aspect that must be carefully managed is narrative coherence. Regardless of the decisions made by the player, the narrative should always remain consistent, engaging, and fulfilling. Maintaining this sense of narrative coherence is particularly challenging in adventure games, where player freedom is a central feature. Yet, it is this challenge that lies at the heart of creating truly immersive interactive experiences.

Strategies for maintaining narrative coherence often involve clever design tactics that create the illusion of freedom while subtly guiding the player along a predetermined narrative path. This can be achieved through techniques such as 'invisible walls', where players are given a wide range of choices, but all roads ultimately lead to the same narrative conclusion. Alternatively, 'branching narratives' can be used, where multiple narrative paths are available, but each one is meticulously crafted to ensure narrative coherence.

Ultimately, maintaining narrative coherence in adventure games is a balancing act between player freedom and authorial control. While players should be given the liberty to make meaningful choices, these choices should not derail the narrative or lead to nonsensical outcomes. The art of interactive storytelling lies in crafting narratives that adapt and react to player choices while maintaining a sense of overall narrative coherence. By achieving this balance, game designers can create truly immersive and compelling interactive narratives.

7.5 Case Study: Balancing Freedom and Narrative in Popular Games

Our journey towards understanding the equilibrium between player freedom and narrative leads us to some of the most successful games in the industry. These games serve as excellent examples of how autonomy and story can coexist harmoniously, creating experiences that are both immersive and engaging. By examining these examples, we can extract valuable lessons and insights.

Let's start with 'The Witcher 3: Wild Hunt', a game widely acclaimed for its narrative depth and player freedom. Players have the liberty to explore a vast, open world, filled with quests and activities. However, despite this freedom, the game maintains a strong central narrative that keeps the player invested. The choices made by players have tangible consequences, yet the core story remains coherent and engaging, demonstrating a perfect harmony between freedom and narrative.

Another stellar example is 'Red Dead Redemption 2'. This game offers an expansive open world, where players can choose to follow the main storyline or veer off into numerous side activities. Yet, even with such broad freedom, the game never loses sight of its narrative. Each choice leads to a new narrative branch, but the overarching story stays consistent and compelling. The player's choices matter, but they never compromise the narrative structure.

These case studies highlight the fact that balancing player freedom and narrative is not only possible but can also lead to remarkable gaming experiences. The key lies in allowing players to make meaningful choices while ensuring that these choices contribute to a cohesive and engaging narrative. As we have seen, when this balance is struck, it results in games that are immensely satisfying, immersive, and memorable.

Chapter 8: The Future of Adventure Games

The best way to predict the future is to
create it. - Peter Drucker

8.1 Emerging Technologies

As we begin to navigate the terrain of the future of adventure games, we cannot ignore the enormous potential of emerging technologies. Virtual Reality (VR), Augmented Reality (AR), and Artificial Intelligence (AI) are not just buzzwords—they are game-changers that are gradually redefining the landscape of gaming. These technologies promise a new dimension of immersion, transforming the way we interact with game environments and characters. In this new era, they are not just enhancing the gaming experience, but they are also redefining what it means to play an adventure game.

Virtual Reality, with its ability to transport players into three-dimensional, fully interactive worlds, is a powerful tool for adventure games. It allows us to step beyond the confines of our screens and into the game world itself. Imagine walking through the labyrinthine corridors of a haunted mansion or scaling the heights of a treacherous mountain—all from the comfort of your living room. This level of immersion could revolutionize the way we experience adventure games, making every choice, every challenge, and every victory feel profoundly real.

Augmented Reality, on the other hand, brings the adventure into our world. It overlays digital elements onto our physical environment, turning our surroundings into an interactive playground. This technology takes the concept of immersive gaming to a whole new level by integrating the game into our everyday lives. Imagine your morning commute turning into a quest, or your local park transforming into a mystical forest filled with puzzles and challenges. The possibilities are endless.

Then there's Artificial Intelligence, a technology that's transforming the way we interact with game characters. AI allows for dynamic, responsive characters that can adapt to the player's actions and decisions. These characters can learn, evolve, and react in ways that were previously unimaginable. This level of realism could make adventure games more engaging, adding depth and complexity to the narrative.

In conclusion, emerging technologies like VR, AR, and AI are not just shaping the future of adventure games, they are revolutionizing it. These technologies allow us to experience games in ways that were once only a figment of our imagination. As these technologies continue to evolve, so too will adventure games. The future of the genre is bound to be as exciting and unpredictable as the games themselves.

8.2 Adventures Beyond the Screen

Adventure games have always offered us a chance to escape, to step into other worlds and live out incredible stories. But what if these adventures could break free from the confines of our screens? What if they could become a part of our physical world, enhancing our reality instead of replacing it? In this section, we'll explore how adventure games are beginning to blur the lines between digital and physical, and what this could mean for the future of the genre.

The integration of adventure games into our physical world is made possible by advancements in technology, particularly augmented reality (AR) and location-based technologies. These innovations allow game developers to overlay digital elements onto our physical environment, creating immersive experiences that bridge the gap between the real and virtual. Imagine exploring your city as a sprawling game map, or finding hidden treasures in your own backyard. The possibilities for adventure are only limited by our imagination.

However, this integration also presents unique challenges for game designers. They must consider how to design games that are engaging and fun, while also being respectful of the real-world environments they inhabit. This requires a delicate balance, blending digital and physical elements in a way that enhances, rather than detracts from, our everyday experiences. It's a challenging task, but one that has the potential to redefine adventure games as we know them.

As we look to the future, we can expect adventure games to continue breaking free from the confines of our screens. They will integrate more seamlessly into our physical world, offering us novel and immersive experiences. This evolution presents fascinating opportunities for game designers and players alike. Indeed, the adventure game of the future might be one that we live, not just one that we play.

8.3   The Rise of Interactive Cinema

The convergence of film and gaming is not a new concept, but its potential has only begun to be realized. Interactive cinema represents a thrilling evolution of this idea, combining the visual spectacle of film with the agency and interactivity of gaming. As this form of entertainment gains popularity, it's worth asking: what impact will it have on adventure games? This section will delve into the rise of interactive cinema and its potential implications for the genre.

The rise of interactive cinema is a testament to the increasing demand for engaging, immersive experiences. This form of storytelling allows for a level of player involvement that was previously unattainable in traditional cinema. Now, viewers can shape the narrative, making decisions that impact the story's direction and outcome. This blurring of boundaries between viewer and participant, between passive and active engagement, presents exciting possibilities for the future of adventure games.

However, the incorporation of interactive cinema into adventure games is not without its challenges. Balancing the visual and narrative complexity of cinema with the interactive demands of gaming requires a careful, thoughtful approach. Moreover, the technological requirements for delivering such experiences are significant. Yet, despite these challenges, the potential rewards—profoundly engaging games that offer a seamless blend of cinematic visuals and interactive gameplay—are substantial.

Interactive cinema is a burgeoning field that holds great promise for the future of adventure games. By blending the narrative strength of cinema with the interactive nature of gaming, we can create experiences that are profoundly engaging and deeply personal. As filmmakers and game designers continue to explore this convergence, we can expect to see truly innovative and groundbreaking adventure games. The stage is set for a new era of interactive storytelling.

8.4 New Narrative Forms

As we peer into the future of adventure games, we find a landscape teeming with exciting innovations. One revolutionary change we're witnessing is the emergence of new narrative forms and structures. These are not just changes in the way we construct our stories, but they represent fundamental shifts in the way we perceive and interact with narratives. The advent of these new forms, facilitated by technological advancements, has the potential to redefine the genre of adventure games, offering players unprecedented control over their narrative journeys.

One such innovation is the development of non-linear narratives. Unlike traditional storytelling, which follows a set path from beginning to end, non-linear narratives allow players to carve their own path through the narrative landscape. This form of storytelling provides a level of engagement that was previously unattainable, as players are not just passive recipients of the story, but active participants in its unfolding. This shift towards non-linearity in narrative design is a direct response to the evolving expectations of gamers who crave more control and agency in their gaming experiences.

Another exciting development is the advent of multiperspective narratives. In these narratives, the story is experienced from multiple viewpoints, offering a more comprehensive and immersive experience. This form of storytelling allows for a level of depth and complexity that adds a new layer of engagement to adventure games. By employing multiple perspectives, game designers can create richer, more nuanced narratives that resonate deeply with players.

8.5   The Social Dimension of Adventure Games

The rise of social media and online communities has transformed the way we experience games. No longer are players isolated entities, navigating through virtual landscapes alone. Instead, they are members of a global community, connected through shared experiences, strategies, and narratives. This shift towards a more social gaming experience is having a profound impact on the design and development of adventure games.

As players become more connected, adventure games are being shaped to reflect this new reality. Developers are incorporating features that allow for more interaction and collaboration between players. Some are even taking it a step further, creating games that evolve based on the collective decisions of the player community. This social dimension is not just changing the way games are designed, but also how they are played.

However, this increasing interconnectedness also presents new challenges. How do developers balance the individual player's agency with the collective will of the community? How do they manage the diverse range of player responses and ensure a coherent narrative? These are the questions that game designers will need to grapple with as they navigate the social future of adventure games.

8.6 Looking Ahead: Predictions and Possibilities

Peering into the future of adventure games, we find a landscape rich with potential. The rapid pace of technological advancements, coupled with evolving player expectations, promises to drive the genre into uncharted territories. While it's impossible to predict with certainty what the future holds, we can make educated guesses based on current trends and innovations. In this final section, we'll speculate on the possibilities that lie ahead for adventure games.

One possibility is the development of adventure

games that are ever more immersive and realistic, thanks to advancements in technology. Virtual reality and augmented reality could provide players with experiences that are indistinguishable from reality, allowing them to literally step into the shoes of their characters. We could also see an increase in the use of artificial intelligence, which could create characters and narratives that adapt and respond to the player's actions in real-time.

Moreover, the future might hold a shift in how we perceive the concept of gaming itself. As the line between gaming and other forms of media continues to blur, we might see adventure games that are not just played, but lived. This could involve games that integrate seamlessly into our everyday lives, transforming our reality into an interactive narrative.

Looking ahead, the future of adventure games is as exciting as it is uncertain. Technological advancements and evolving player expectations will continue to drive the genre forward, into uncharted territories. While we can't predict exactly what this future will look like, we can be sure it will be filled with innovative ideas, immersive experiences, and thrilling adventures. The key to the door of this future is in our hands, and we cannot wait to unlock it.

Conclusion: The Key to the Door

The only impossible journey is the one you
never begin. - Tony Robbins

9.1 Recap: The Essence of Interactive Story-telling

As we cross the threshold one last time, it's essential to revisit the core principles that underpin the art of interactive storytelling. Remember, the essence of this genre lies in the interplay of player choices, branching narratives, and engaging game design. These elements should not only entertain but also engage players on a deeper, emotional level, stirring their curiosity and sparking their imagination.

The power of interactive storytelling stems from its ability to create a unique bond between the player and the narrative. By allowing players to influence the course of the story, adventure games forge a deeply personal connection that traditional linear narratives cannot replicate. This connection magnifies the emotional impact of the narrative, making the player an integral part of the story rather than a passive observer.

We end this journey where we began, at the heart of interactive storytelling—the player and their choices. As you move forward, keep these principles at the forefront of your design process. Remember, the success of your game hinges not on its complexity, but on how compellingly it engages the player in the narrative journey. And in this journey, every choice, every branch, every puzzle, and every character plays a vital role.

9.2 Adventure Games: A Unique Narrative Medium

Adventure games offer a unique narrative platform unlike any other. They provide fertile ground for stories that can evolve and change based on player actions. This interactive dimension allows for a level of immersion and engagement that traditional linear narratives simply cannot achieve. By leveraging these unique qualities, you can craft experiences that resonate deeply with players and leave a lasting impression.

The beauty of adventure games lies in their inherent flexibility. The narrative structure allows for a multitude of branching paths, creating a myriad of possible outcomes determined by the player's choices. This means that each player's experience can be entirely distinct, fostering a deep sense of personal investment and ownership over the story. This sense of agency is what sets adventure games apart from other narrative mediums.

Moreover, adventure games offer an unparalleled platform for exploring complex themes and ideas. The ability to embed moral dilemmas and philosophical questions within the gameplay itself can provoke thought and reflection in a way that passive consumption of media cannot. The player's active involvement in the narrative progression allows for a deeper engagement with these themes, making them more impactful and memorable.

In the world of adventure games, the line between reality and fiction often blurs. The immersive nature of these games can create a profound emotional connection between the player and the narrative. The choices made in the game world often reflect the player's own values and beliefs, further deepening their engagement with the story. This level of personal involvement and emotional resonance is a testament to the power of adventure games as a narrative medium.

In conclusion, the unique qualities of adventure games afford them a special place in the realm of storytelling. They offer a narrative experience that is immersive, engaging, and deeply personal. By understanding and harnessing these qualities, you can create compelling stories that leave a lasting impression on your players. Remember, in the world of adventure games, you're not just telling a story—you're crafting an experience.

9.3   Your Role as a Game Writer

As a game writer, you are not just a storyteller—you are a world-builder, a character-creator, a decision-designer. Your role is pivotal in shaping the player's journey through the interactive narrative. You are tasked with the delicate balance of guiding the narrative while still providing ample room for player agency. This responsibility is both daunting and exhilarating, and it's what makes game writing such a unique and rewarding craft.

The choices you make as a game writer reverberate throughout the game world, influencing not only the course of the narrative but also the player's experience. Every decision point, every dialogue, every plot twist springs from your mind, shaping the contours of the adventure. It's a form of storytelling that's collaborative in nature, involving a dialogue between the game designer, the player, and the world you've created. The power of your words can build worlds, breathe life into characters, and forge unforgettable journeys.

But this power comes with a responsibility. The narratives you weave have the potential to deeply impact players, influencing their perceptions and emotions. As a game writer, you have the opportunity to create meaningful, thought-provoking experiences that can resonate with players long after they've put the game down. It's a task that requires a deep understanding of narrative structure, character development, and the art of interactive storytelling.

In the end, the role of a game writer transcends the boundaries of traditional storytelling. You are a key player in a dynamic, ever-evolving narrative landscape, steering the player's journey while responding to their choices and actions. It's a role that blends creativity with strategy, imagination with structure. As you embrace this role, remember to cherish the unique challenges and rewards it brings. After all, you are not just writing a story—you are creating an immersive, interactive experience.

9.4   The Future of Interactive Storytelling

Looking ahead, the future of interactive storytelling holds immense potential. With the advent of emerging technologies like virtual and augmented reality, the realm of adventure games is on the brink of unprecedented evolution. This evolution not only presents exciting new possibilities for game design but also challenges us to continuously adapt and innovate. As we push the boundaries of this medium, our narratives will become ever more immersive, engaging, and intricate.

The evolution of interactive storytelling is not just about technological advancements but also about the changing expectations of players. Today's players desire more than just mind-bending puzzles and intricate storylines—they want to be active participants in the narrative, shaping the story with their choices. This calls for more nuanced game design, where the narrative evolves organically based on player actions, making each playthrough a unique experience.

Moreover, the rise of social and multiplayer gaming is adding a new dimension to interactive storytelling. Now, narratives are not just shaped by individual choices but also by the collective decisions of a group of players. This presents a unique challenge and opportunity for game writers—to create stories that are not only dynamic and responsive but also foster social interaction and collaboration.

Another trend shaping the future of adventure games is the increasing use of artificial intelligence. AI can be used to create more dynamic and responsive game environments, where the world itself can adapt and respond to player actions. This can further enhance player immersion and make the game world feel truly alive.

In conclusion, the future of interactive storytelling is bright and full of possibilities. With the convergence of technological advancements and evolving player expectations, we are on the cusp of a new era in adventure gaming. As game writers, it's our responsibility and privilege to explore these new frontiers and continue pushing the boundaries of what's possible. So, let's look forward to the future, embrace the challenges, and continue crafting immersive, engaging, and meaningful interactive narratives.

9.5   Final Thoughts: Unlocking the Door

In conclusion, this book has armed you with the knowledge and tools necessary to craft your own adventure games. The journey may be challenging, but remember—it's also an opportunity to create something truly unique and impactful. The key to successful interactive storytelling is now in your hands. So, start unlocking doors, and let your creative journey begin.

Embrace the challenges that come with creating interactive narratives. Each obstacle you encounter is an opportunity to learn and grow as a game writer. Trust in the process, and remember that even the most complex narratives start with a single choice. Your adventure game is waiting to be written; all it needs is for you to take the first step.

As you embark on this journey, remember to keep your players at the heart of your narrative decisions. Strive to create experiences that captivate, challenge, and evoke emotion. Your story has the potential to transport players into a world of your making, influencing their thoughts, feelings, and decisions in profound ways.

Finally, be bold in your storytelling. Push the boundaries of what's possible in interactive narratives. Experiment with new ideas, take risks, and never stop exploring the vast potential of this medium. The future of adventure games is in your hands, and it's waiting for you to shape it.